W9-ANP-613

Planet
Earth

JOURNEY
INTO SPACE

MICHAEL BRIGHT

PowerKiDS
press™

Published in 2018 by **The Rosen Publishing Group, Inc.**
29 East 21st Street, New York, NY 10010

Cataloging-in-Publication Data
Names: Bright, Michael.
Title: Journey into space / Michael Bright.
Description: New York : PowerKids Press, 2018. | Series: Planet Earth | Includes index.
Identifiers: ISBN 9781508153993 (pbk.) | ISBN 9781508153931 (library bound) | ISBN 9781508153825 (6 pack)
Subjects: LCSH: Astronomy--Juvenile literature. | Outer space--Exploration--Juvenile literature.
Classification: LCC TL793.B69 2018 | DDC 629.4--dc23

Written by Michael Bright
Cover illustration by Mark Turner
Editor: Corinne Lucas
Designer: Alyssa Peacock

Picture credits: P 4 (t) © Everett Historical /Shutterstock; P 4 (b) © NASA; P 5 (t) © Wikimedia Commons; P 5 (b) © Sovfoto/ Contributor/Getty Images; P 6 (t) © NASA/Marshall Space Flight Center; P 6 (b) © Bettmann/Getty Images; P 7 (t) © NASA; P 7 (m) © NASA; P 7 (b) © NASA; P 8 © NASA; P 9 (t) © NASA; P 9 (b) © NASA; P 10 © NASA; P 11 (t) © NASA; P 11 (m) © NASA; P 11 (b) © NASA; P 12 © NASA; P 13 (t) © NASA; P 13 (m) © NASA; P 13 (b) © ESA-AOES Medialab; P 14 (t) © Vadim Sadovski/ Shutterstock; p 14 (b) © NASA; P 15 (t) © NASA/JPL-Caltech/MSSS; P 15 (b) © NASA; P 16 © NASA; P 17 (t) © NASA; P 17 (b) © NASA; P 18 © NASA; P 19 (t) © NASA/JPL-Caltech/Space Science Institute; P 19 (b) © NASA/JPL/SSI; P 19 © NASA; P 20 © Lunar Planetary Institute; P 21 (t) © mr.Timmi/shutterstock; P 21 (m) © NASA; P 21 (b) © NASA; P 22 © AvDe/Shutterstock; P 23 (t) © NASA/JPL-Caltech/UMD; P 23 (b) © NASA; P 24 (t) © NASA/JPL/JHUAPL; P 24 (b) © BSIP/UIG/Getty Images; P 25 (t) © NASA/JPL-Caltech/UCLA/MPS/DLR/IDA; P 25 (b) © Wikimedia Commons; P 26 (t) © Aphelleon/Shutterstock; P 26 (b) © NASA/Johns Hopkins University Applied Physics Laboratory/Southwest Research Institute; P 27 (t) © NASA; P 27 (b) © NASA/ INTERNEGATIVE/SCIENCE PHOTO LIBRARY; P 28 (t) © P.G.ADAM,PUBLIPHOTO DIFFUSION/SCIENCE PHOTO LIBRARY; P 28 (b) © Richard Bizley/Science Photo Library; P 29 (t) © ESA/NASA/SOHO; P 29 (b) © AF archive / Alamy Stock Photo;

Manufactured in China

CPSIA Compliance Information: Batch #BS17PK: For Further Information contact Rosen Publishing, New York, New York at 1-800-237-9932.

contents

the SPACE RACE

For centuries, people have dreamed of traveling into outer space. They have been fascinated by fictional space adventurers who hurtle through the **atmosphere** at great speeds and encounter alien creatures from other worlds. Now, space travel is a reality, and alien worlds are within reach!

rocket war

During the 1940s, Nazi Germany developed the V-2 rocket, which could be flown over the English Channel to bomb London. It was the first long-range **ballistic missile**, but on one occasion it played a purely scientific role. On June 20, 1944, a V-2 rocket was sent vertically upwards to become the first man-made object to leave the Earth's atmosphere and reach outer space.

Successful launch of a German V-2 rocket in 1943.

space race is on

After World War II, Germany's V-2 rocket experts were captured. Some went to work for the USA and others went to what was then the USSR (Russia). It was the start of the "space race" between the two superpowers. The USSR won on October 4, 1957, when it put the first man-made **satellite** into **Earth orbit**. It was a shiny, round sphere with four radio antennae. They called it Sputnik.

first animals in space

Animals were launched aboard rockets to test how living things might survive in the weightlessness of space and how **cosmic rays** might affect them. On February 20, 1947, the first animals in space were fruit flies riding on top of a US-launched V-2 rocket. Mice, rabbits, rats, guinea pigs, frogs, dogs, monkeys, and apes followed them.

Veterok and Ugoljok spent 22 days in space in 1966, the longest space flight for any dog.

Laika was the first Earth-born animal to orbit the Earth.

dogs in space

The first large animals to travel into space were dogs. In 1951, Tsygan and Dezik were launched into space on a Russian rocket. They did not orbit the Earth, but they were successfully recovered alive and well. In 1957, a dog called Laika orbited the Earth in Sputnik 2, the first animal to do so, but she died in space because the technology to bring her back had not been invented yet.

5

manned
SPACE FLIGHT

In the early days, so little was known about space, space travel, and its effects on the body, it was essential to test how humans would respond to the challenging conditions beyond the Earth. Before there could be a manned flight, the closest things — monkeys and apes — had to make the journey for us so we could learn more.

Monkey Baker with a model of the Jupiter rocket that took it into space.

rocket monkeys

The first monkey to reach outer space was Albert II. Many more monkeys followed him through the US space program. Some died, but others returned successfully to Earth. This showed that monkeys could survive the high speeds of the launch, weightlessness in space, and re-entry at 10,000 mph (16,000 kph). It meant that people could probably survive, too.

apes in space

Humans are distantly related to chimpanzees, so they became the perfect space-travel testers. Ham the chimpanzee was the first. In 1961, he was taken into space in the **capsule**, Mercury. He was trained to pull levers and showed that tasks could be performed during the weightlessness of a space flight. He returned safely to the Earth and lived for 17 years in Washington's National Zoo.

first human in space

When humans decided to go into outer space, the Russian **cosmonaut** Yuri Gagarin was the first. He entered the Vostok 1 space capsule on April 12, 1961, and was blasted into Earth's orbit. He was the first human to travel in space, orbiting the Earth just once in a flight that lasted 108 minutes.

first humans on the moon

Russia successfully launched both the first man and, in 1963, the first woman — Valentina Tereshkova — into space. The USA kept the space race alive with a series of manned space flights that eventually landed the first man on the Moon. On July 20, 1969, US astronaut Neil Armstrong lowered himself from the ladder on the side of the moon lander and stepped onto the **lunar** surface with the memorable words "One small step for man, one giant leap for mankind."

Apollo 11 Mission Commander Neil Armstrong during the first working session on the Moon.

Space
STATIONS

The National Aeronautics and Space Administration (NASA) ran the US space program and its Project Apollo to put people on the Moon. The crews were mainly military test pilots, and Apollo 11 was the first to land on the moon. However, it was not until Apollo 17 that a scientist went on a mission. This was the start of doing experiments in space.

Scientists in space

Scientists needed a laboratory in space to do their experiments so they built space stations. The first space station, called Salyut 1, was launched by the USSR for scientific research. NASA's first space station was Skylab. It was sent into orbit in 1973 and it was almost a disaster. Parts of the station were torn off during launch, but the crew (who were following in another spacecraft) were able to repair it. Skylab contained a workshop and instruments to study the Sun. It remained in orbit with a constantly changing three-person crew for six years, proving that people could carry out work in the weightlessness of space for long periods of time.

Spacelab was a laboratory carried in the Space Shuttle's hold during special research flights.

long-term space living

NASA's Space Shuttle *Atlantic* docking with the Russian Mir space station.

The Russian Mir Space Station was launched in 1986. It had several sections, each sent up separately on rockets. Crews and food arrived by *Soyuz* spacecraft, which docked with the space station. It was used for more than a decade and showed that human outposts in space could be maintained over long periods of time — one step towards living permanently in space.

largest man-made body in space

The latest and biggest space station is the International Space Station. The first section was launched in 1998, the first crew arrived in 2000, and it has been continually occupied ever since.

Eating and drinking in space is not straightforward because everything floats around. Crews must be careful not to create crumbs because they could block the air filters. Drinks and soups are sucked from plastic bags with straws, and solid food is eaten normally using knives and forks.

A cosmonaut tackles a hamburger and tomato in space.

THE EDGE of the UNIVERSE

For **astronomers** and **cosmologists**, the exciting thing about carrying out science experiments in space is taking special telescopes into Earth's orbit. They can then observe the universe without the images being distorted by the Earth's atmosphere or blotted out by the glare of **light pollution** from cities on the Earth's surface.

hubble space telescope

The Space Shuttle *Discovery* launched in 1990, carrying a telescope named after the American astronomer, Edwin Hubble (1889–1953). The Hubble Space Telescope can look at faint **galaxies** that are **billions** of **light-years** away, at the very edge of the universe. These galaxies would have been made not long after the **Big Bang**, so by studying them, scientists can work out the age and size of the universe. They believe the universe is 13.8 billion years old, and the tiny bit of it we can see is at least 91 billion light-years across — and getting bigger.

An astronaut on a "space walk" services the Hubble Space Telescope.

Kepler's mission is to search for exoplanets.

SPACE SHUTTLE

The Space Shuttle was NASA's first reusable space transport — a "space truck." It took off like a rocket, but landed like an aircraft. It was one of the transport vehicles used to build and maintain the International Space Station, and it carried scientific satellites, such the Chandra X-ray Observatory, into Earth orbit. Amongst many other things, Chandra has recorded "burping" black holes. A black hole is an area of space that has such strong gravity that it sucks in everything else around it, including stars and their solar systems.

kepler space telescope

NASA's Kepler Space Telescope was named after the German astronomer Johannes Kepler (1571–1630). It was launched by a Delta II rocket in 2009, and it has helped scientists to find **exoplanets** in **solar systems** around distant stars. Sun-like stars with Earth-like planets that are in the "habitable zone" — the distance from the star where liquid water can gather on the planet's surface — are of particular interest. Water is essential for life as we know it. Observations from Kepler reveal that there are at least 11 billion Earth-like planets in our Milky Way galaxy alone, the nearest being about 12 light-years away.

close to THE SUN

While sending astronauts to the Moon is possible, traveling to the other planets in our solar system is much harder. The distances between planets are enormous and current spacecraft travel too slowly. The answer is to send unmanned spacecraft instead. Some take years to reach their destinations.

close to the Sun

In 1974, NASA's *Mariner 10* was the first spacecraft to get close to Mercury, the nearest planet to the Sun. It revealed that Mercury has a Moon-like surface with **craters** and a thin atmosphere made mainly of the gas helium. Mercury also experiences extraordinary temperatures. In the most extreme places at the **equator**, the daytime temperature can be up to 800°F (427°C), but the nighttime temperature plunges to -197°F (-183°C). Despite the high daytime temperature, in 2011, NASA's Messenger probe discovered water-ice in craters that were permanently in shadow.

Mercury's surface has wrinkles, each wrinkle over a mile high and hundreds of miles long.

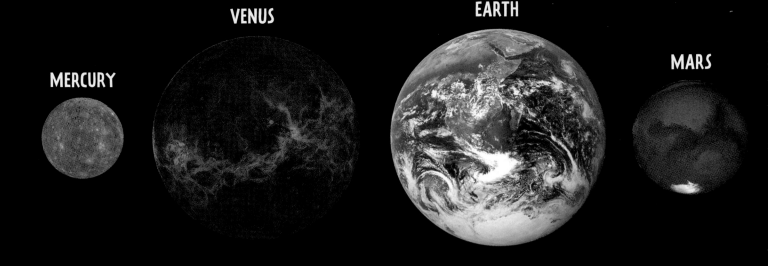

MERCURY VENUS EARTH MARS

eccentric planet

Mercury is the smallest planet in our solar system. Unlike the others Mercury spins very slowly. At first, it was thought that the same side faced the Sun all the time, but observations have revealed that a day on Mercury is the equivalent of 176 Earth days. It is a world of extremely long days and nights!

planetary hothouse

Russia's *Venera 4* and *7* were the first space probes to send back data on Venus. They found that its extremely thick atmosphere is 97% carbon dioxide, creating an extreme **greenhouse effect**. The result is that the air temperature at the surface is a staggering 887°F (475°C), even hotter than Mercury.

Several countries were involved in another mission called Vega. It floated two weather balloons into the atmosphere and found hurricane-force winds, clouds of sulphuric acid, and an **atmospheric pressure** on the surface that is similar to being at the bottom of the deep sea on Earth.

Thick clouds obscure the surface of Venus.

ESA's Venus Express spacecraft

the red
PLANET

Our neighbor Mars has attracted lots of attention, especially because space agencies are considering a manned mission to the planet (see pages 28–29). Also, because it is possible that simple life-forms might be found there.

mars rovers

In 1971, NASA's Mariner 9 was the first spacecraft to orbit a planet when it orbited Mars. Mars 3 was the first spacecraft to land gently there. Then, in 1997, Sojourner was the first motorized rover to drive across the surface, followed in 2004 by Spirit and Opportunity, and in

water features

Mars's two moons have found that there is ice at the poles and quantities of water in the surface soil.

Curiosity rover on Mount Sharp on Mars.

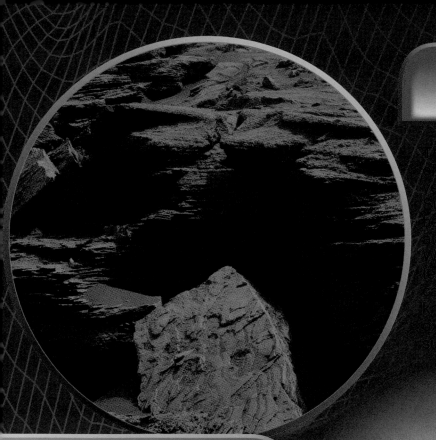

dust storms

The seasons on Mars are twice the length of those on Earth, because its Martian year is twice as long as Earth's. In summer, temperatures at the equator can reach $86°F$ ($30°C$), but winter temperatures at the poles can be $-205°F$ ($-130°C$). When Mars is closer to the Sun and the temperature rises, gigantic dust storms can sweep across the atmosphere. It is known as the 'red planet' because iron oxide (rust) dust is widespread on its surface, giving it a reddish tinge.

majestic geography

Mars is rocky, like the Earth, and it has a cold, desert-like surface and thin atmosphere. It also has some of the largest canyons in the solar system – the 2,485-mile-long (4,000-km) and 4.4-mile-deep (7-km) Valles Marineris – and the highest volcano, Olympus Mons. At 14 miles (22 km) high, it is nearly three times the height of Mount Everest.

A great dust storm on Mars.

The surface of Mars has a distinctly red tinge.

KING of the PLANETS

The first mission to Jupiter was in 1973 by NASA's *Pioneer 10*, but soon after it became the solar system's most visited planet. Space probes use its **gravitational pull** to steer through the solar system. It even causes the spacecraft to go faster, while actually using less fuel. Mission crews call this a "slingshot."

failed star

Jupiter is a "gas giant" and the largest planet in the solar system. Instead of being solid — like the Earth and Mars — it is made mainly of gases, such as hydrogen and helium. This makes it similar to the Sun, but it did not grow big enough to become a star. Deep in the planet the pressure is so great that the hydrogen gas probably becomes liquid, forming the biggest "ocean" in the solar system, made of hydrogen rather than water. It might also have a rocky core about the size of the Earth, although nobody is sure.

striped planet

Seen from the Earth or from a spacecraft, Jupiter's outer atmosphere appears to be made of colorful bands. Along the edges between the bands there are violent storms blowing at 224 miles per hour (360 kph). The Great Red Spot is a complex storm, two to three times as wide as the Earth, which has been raging for nearly 400 years! Its winds move in a counterclockwise direction at speeds of at least 336 miles per hour (540 kph).

Jupiter is 2.5 times bigger than all the other planets combined!

jupiter's rings

In 1979, *Voyager 1* discovered Jupiter has a faint ring around it. The outer rings are called gossamer rings and the thicker inner rings are known as halos. In 2000, the *Cassini* spacecraft found that the particles in the rings were not round but irregular in shape, suggesting they are made of the **debris** left over from collisions between **meteorites** and Jupiter's moons.

The white line marks where Jupiter's faint, 18.5-mile-wide (30 km) ring system is located.

Io

Europa

Ganymede

Callisto

many moons

Jupiter could have as many as 67 moons, so it's like a miniature version of the solar system. The largest moons are Ganymede, Io, Europa, and Callisto. Ganymede is the largest — it's bigger than the planet Mercury. Io has active volcanoes, and Europa has a **crust** of frozen water on its surface, below which is possibly an ocean 30 miles (50 km) deep. Callisto is half rock and half ice, with a thin atmosphere made of the gas carbon dioxide.

JEWEL in the SOLAR SYSTEM

After a slingshot around Jupiter, NASA's *Pioneer 11* was the first space probe to reach Saturn in 1979. It flew through Saturn's rings, testing the way for obstacles so later spacecraft could follow safely. The *Pioneer 11* discovered new moons, almost colliding with one, bringing Saturn's total known moons to 62.

Ring particles range in size from grains of dust to a few the size of mountains!

ringed planet

Saturn is the sixth planet from the Sun. Like Jupiter, it is a gas giant, mainly made of hydrogen and helium. It has seven distinct rings. The rings extend hundreds of thousands of miles (km) from the planet, yet they are between 30 feet (10 m) and 0.6 mile (1 km) thick. They are made mostly of lumps of ice.

violent storms

The *Voyager 1* probe was sent to Saturn in 1980. It found winds blowing at 1,100 miles per hour (1,770 kph). In 2004, the *Cassini-Huygens* spacecraft recorded the aftermath of a storm, named the Great White Spot, which occurs in Saturn's northern hemisphere every 30 years. The storm was 149°F (83°C) hotter than its surroundings, which were -334°F (-130°C).

Titan is bigger than the planet Mercury.

methane lakes

Saturn's largest moon, Titan, is interesting to scientists because it has a nitrogen-rich atmosphere that could be similar to Earth's early atmosphere, but it is thought to be too cold for life. The moon is flat, with hills no higher than 165 ft (50 m), and there appear to be lakes and even seas, not made of water, but of **methane** and **ethane**, under a surface of ice.

About 100 ice geysers eject water vapor, ice, and common salt crystals.

ice fountains

One of Saturn's other moons, Enceladus, has ice **geysers** erupting near its south pole. Pockets of liquid water near the surface could be fueling the eruptions, and the material thrown into space could be helping to form one of Saturn's rings. There is also evidence of a large, salty ocean below the moon's surface. It is one of the most likely places outside of the Earth that alien **microbes** could live.

the
ICE GIANTS

Voyager 2 is the only spacecraft to have visited all of the outer planets, including the two enormous planets outside the orbit of Saturn — Uranus and Neptune. They are known as the "ice giants" because out there towards the edge of the solar system it is cold — really cold. The surface of Uranus is generally about -350°F (-212°C).

the blue-green planet

Like Jupiter and Saturn, Uranus is composed mainly of hydrogen and helium, along with a core of icy liquid methane, water, and ammonium. Its green-blue color comes from the methane in its atmosphere. Methane takes in the red light from sunlight, but reflects blue light back into space, so the planet looks bluish-green. It has 13 rings and 27 moons. Miranda is the most unusual moon with canyons 12 miles (20 km) deep.

Neptune

Uranus

Earth

temperature extremes

A Uranus day is 17 Earth hours, so it is not unlike our day, but its year is the equivalent of 84 Earth years. Also, Uranus is on its side and rotates horizontally, rather than vertically like the other planets. This means that during every 20-year-long season, parts of the planet are either in almost continuous sunlight or darkness. However, it is so far from the Sun that it never gets warm.

the bright blue planet

Neptune was discovered in 1846, but it did not complete an orbit of the Sun until 2011, which means the Neptune year is 165 Earth-years long. It shares the position of outermost planet of the solar system with the dwarf planet Pluto. Their orbits overlap. Like Uranus, Neptune has methane in its atmosphere so it appears blue, but some other, unknown gas in its atmosphere gives it a more intense blue color.

Neptune has swirling storms called great dark spots.

icy moon

Neptune's largest moon, Triton, orbits the planet in the opposite direction to its other 13 moons, and it is extremely cold there. Temperatures on its surface drop to -391°F (-235°C), yet geysers have been seen to spew icy materials upwards to more than 5 miles (8 km) from the surface. Curiously, Triton's temperature is slowly rising, but nobody knows why.

COMETS

Comets are lumps of ice, dust, and rocky particles that orbit the Sun. The main part, known as the nucleus, sometimes has an atmosphere or "coma," and as the comet melts, it often creates a "tail" of debris trailing on the side that is away from the Sun. Comets can be hundreds of yards (meters) or tens of miles (kilometers) across, and have all kinds of different shapes.

long and short journeys

A comet can take hundreds, and in some cases, millions of years to make a single circuit around the Sun. Most comets with short journeys come from the Kuiper Belt, which is beyond the orbit of Neptune, and many of the comets that take longer to go around the Sun start out in the Oort Cloud. This is close to the edge of the solar system.

Millions of icy and rocky objects make up the Kuiper Belt.

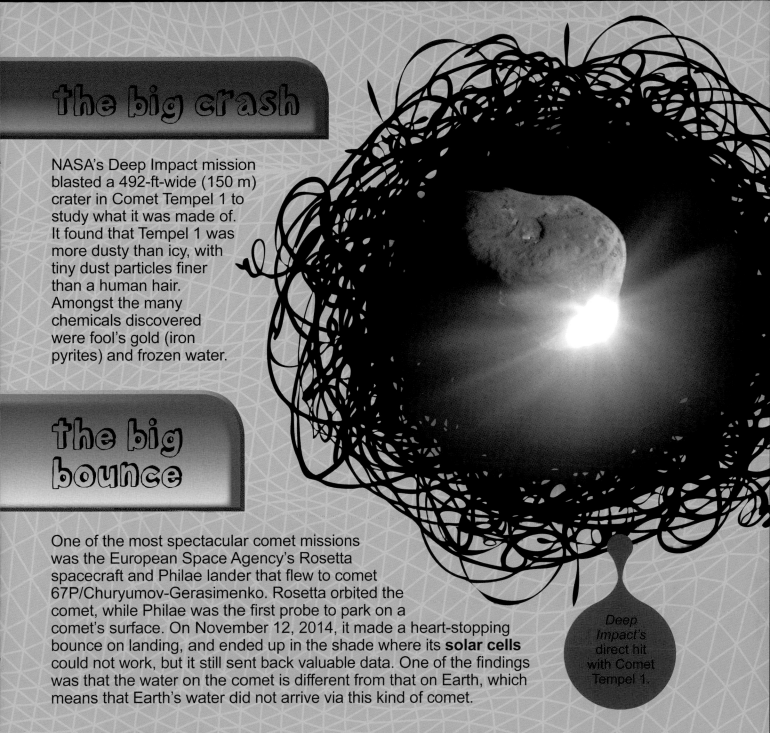

the big crash

NASA's Deep Impact mission blasted a 492-ft-wide (150 m) crater in Comet Tempel 1 to study what it was made of. It found that Tempel 1 was more dusty than icy, with tiny dust particles finer than a human hair. Amongst the many chemicals discovered were fool's gold (iron pyrites) and frozen water.

the big bounce

One of the most spectacular comet missions was the European Space Agency's Rosetta spacecraft and Philae lander that flew to comet 67P/Churyumov-Gerasimenko. Rosetta orbited the comet, while Philae was the first probe to park on a comet's surface. On November 12, 2014, it made a heart-stopping bounce on landing, and ended up in the shade where its **solar cells** could not work, but it still sent back valuable data. One of the findings was that the water on the comet is different from that on Earth, which means that Earth's water did not arrive via this kind of comet.

Deep Impact's direct hit with Comet Tempel 1.

BRINGERS OF BAD NEWS

There are more than 5,250 known comets from the **trillion** that probably exist, and our **ancestors** recognized several of them. These unusually bright comets, clearly seen by the naked eye, are known as the "Great Comets," such as Halley's comet. They were the source of all sorts of ancient predictions, but the message generally was that something terrible was about to happen.

ASTEROIDS

Asteroids are lumps of space rock that include some of the smaller bodies in the solar system. Many are in the asteroid belt, between the orbits of Mars and Jupiter, but a few are elsewhere, such as the near-Earth asteroids. They can vary in size from a few meters across up to 620 miles (1,000 km).

asteroid mining

NASA's Shoemaker space probe flew close to the asteroid Eros, a knobbly, potato-shaped near-Earth asteroid, and touched down on its surface in 2001. This asteroid is interesting because it could crash into the Earth with a similar impact to the asteroid that killed off the dinosaurs. It also could be the source of valuable minerals. It is thought to contain 44,000 billion pounds (20,000 billion kg) of minerals that are rare on Earth, such as aluminium, platinum and gold.

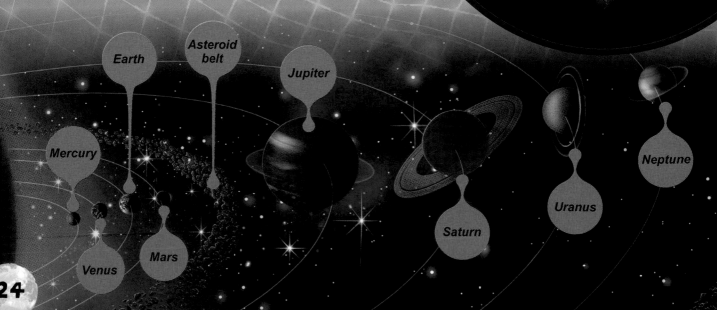

Mercury

Venus

Earth

Mars

Asteroid belt

Jupiter

Saturn

Uranus

Neptune

dwarf planet ceres

The largest asteroids are the dwarf planet Ceres and the protoplanet Vesta. NASA's *Dawn* spacecraft visited them both in 2011–12. Ceres has a rocky core and could have frozen water and clay on its cratered surface, with liquid water below. The Herschel Space Observatory had previously detected a faint atmosphere of water vapor on Ceres. Its craters have bright spots in them, thought to be the Sun reflecting off large patches of ice or salt that have reached the surface from deep below.

A piece of the Millbillillie meteorite that was once part of Vesta.

protoplanet

Vesta is only 355 miles (572 km) across at its widest point, yet it has an enormous crater that is 311 miles (500 km) in **diameter** on its southern side. It was probably the result of a major collision with another space body. Fragments of rock from the crash sometimes arrive on Earth, such as the fireball that streaked across the sky in Millbillillie, Australia, in 1960. Like the rocky planets, Vesta has an iron-nickel core, rocky **mantle**, and a solidified lava crust on the surface. It is an asteroid that did not quite grow into a planet — known as a protoplanet.

PLUTO and BEYOND

Pluto lies in the Kuiper Belt, beyond Neptune. It was once considered to be the ninth planet in the solar system, but as several similar-sized objects have been discovered in the Kuiper Belt, it has been demoted to a dwarf or minor planet. It is so far out, the Sun's light takes about 5.5 hours to reach Pluto, compared to eight minutes and 20 seconds to reach the Earth.

closing in on pluto

After a nine-year journey at a speed of 31,000 miles per hour (50,000 kph), NASA's New Horizons spacecraft had the first close encounter with Pluto and its largest moon, Charon, in 2015. It discovered that Pluto's atmosphere consists mainly of nitrogen, methane and carbon monoxide, and that nitrogen **glaciers** flow across Pluto's surface. There are mountains made of water-ice, possibly volcanoes that spew out water and ice instead of lava, but no impact craters. This means Pluto is either a relatively young planet or its surface is continually changing because of the movements of its rocks, smoothing out any scars.

Pluto is slightly smaller than Earth's moon.

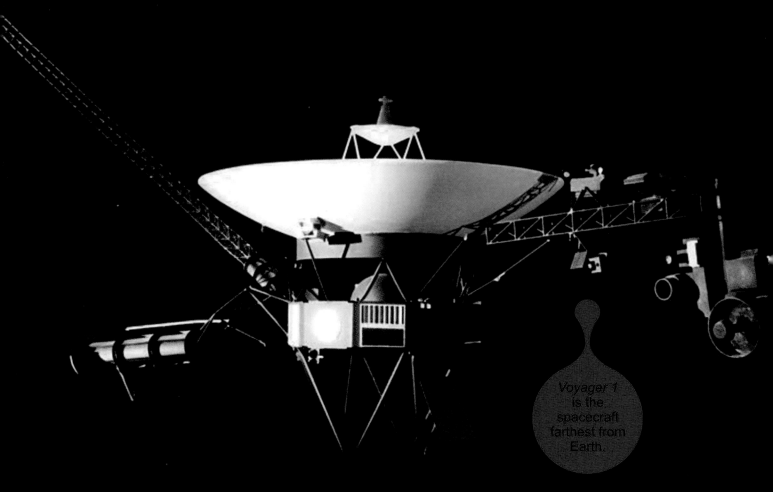

Voyager 1 is the spacecraft farthest from Earth.

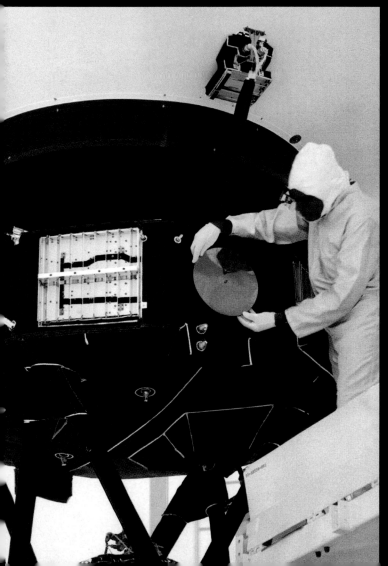

EVERLASTING TRAVELERS

Having completed their work in the solar system, the space probes are heading to outer space. The spacecraft *Voyager 1* is now at the very edge of the solar system in **interstellar space** and, as long as it does not crash into something, it could wander through the Milky Way galaxy almost forever. Should intelligent life-forms find it, the probe carries a gold disc with pictures of the Earth, music, natural sounds, and greetings from Earth's people in 55 different languages. It will reach the Oort Cloud in 300 years and in 40,000 years it will be 1.6 light-years from the star Gliese 445, which itself is 17.6 light-years from our Sun. *Voyager 2*, carrying a second gold disc, and *Pioneer 10* and *11*, are also heading towards interstellar space.

the final FRONTIER

Humans have lived on space stations for up to a year at a time and stayed on the Moon for just three days, but there are plans for even longer journeys and greater goals. These include a base on the Moon and a manned mission to Mars. It means that one day in the future people might live on other planets and moons in the solar system, and even elsewhere in outer space.

moon base

The first time a manned base on the Moon was suggested was in 1638 by John Wilkins, Bishop of Chester. Since then, scientists and politicians have come up with all sorts of suggestions and designs, such as **modular dwellings** sent bit by bit from Earth, and underground caverns dug into the lunar surface. The most recent thinking is that a Moon base could take over from the International Space Station (see pages 8–9) as the place to do scientific experiments in space. It is thought a base could be up and running by about 2030.

The "Biosphere" on Earth **simulates** conditions for a colony on the Moon or Mars.

Martian colony.

destination mars

With current spacecraft, it would take six to seven months to reach Mars from the Earth. Even so, scientists are considering setting up a base there. There is water on the planet, the Martian day is similar to an Earth day, and the seasons are similar to those on the Earth, only twice as long. The biggest problem is that, unlike the Earth, Mars is not protected by a **magnetic field**, so dangerous rays and particles can reach its surface. Any dwellings and places for growing food would need to be underground.

MARS GLOBAL EXPRESS

space storms

The weather on the Moon and on Mars is dependent on the Sun, like the weather on the Earth. Solar flares are flashes of brightness on the Sun's surface that give off clouds of potentially dangerous particles. They're one of the greatest dangers to life in space. They can damage electronic instruments in satellites and spacecraft, and endanger the lives of anybody in space.

Apollo 11 Lunar Module Pilot, Buzz Aldrin.

goodbye earth, hello universe

Outside of the Earth, astronauts are more exposed to the dangers of space weather. Even so, Buzz Aldrin, the second man to walk on the Moon, supports a mission to Mars. He sees the Moon not as a destination, but as a point of departure, and believes that people could settle on Mars just as we have settled all over Earth. Some day, humans may be a "two-planet species."

glossary

ancestor a person to whom we are related who lived in the past

astronomer a scientist who studies stars and planets and other bodies in space

atmosphere the layer of gases surrounding a planet or moon

atmospheric pressure the force that pushes down on the surface of a planet or moon due to the weight of its atmosphere

ballistic missile a rocket flying a particular course that delivers one or more bombs to a target

Big Bang the moment when the universe began

billion one thousand million

capsule a manned spacecraft without wings or any other feature to help it re-enter the Earth's atmosphere

cosmic ray high-energy particles from outer space

cosmologist a scientist who studies the history and structure of the universe

cosmonaut a Russian astronaut

crater a bowl-shaped hole in the top of a volcano or one made by the impact of a large object

crust the hard, rocky outer layer forming a planet's surface

debris scattered remains of something that has broken up

diameter straight line passing through the center of a circle or sphere from one edge to the other

Earth orbit the path of something in space, such as a moon or satellite, flying around the Earth and kept in place by the Earth's gravity

equator an imaginary line around a planet or moon, midway between its north and south poles

ethane a colorless gas found in natural gas on Earth

exoplanet a planet orbiting another star, rather than our Sun

galaxy a group of stars

geyser a spring that squirts out hot water and steam from time to time

glacier a river of solid ice that moves downhill

gravitational pull the force that attracts small objects to large objects

greenhouse effect when heat from the Sun is trapped in the atmosphere by gases, such as carbon dioxide and methane

interstellar space the space between stars

light pollution the artificial light from cities and towns that blocks out the natural light from stars in the sky

light-year the distance light travels in one Earth year

lunar to do with the moon

magnetic field the force, similar to that around a bar magnet with a north and a south pole, that surrounds the Earth

mantle the layer on the inside of a planet that is between the crust and the core

meteorite a small, solid piece from a planet, asteroid or comet that whizzes around the solar system

methane the main gas found in natural gas on Earth

microbe a tiny living thing, including bacteria

modular dwellings houses built of units that can be assembled easily

pole the point at the top or bottom of a planet or moon

satellite a natural or artificial body that orbits a planet or other larger body

simulate imitate the appearance and character of something

solar cell a device used to convert sunlight to electricity

solar system The Sun, planets, moons, comets, asteroids and all the other space bodies under the influence of our star, the Sun

trillion one thousand billion

further information

Books

Exploring Space: From Galileo to the Mars Rover and Beyond (2017)
Martin Jenkins and Stephen Biesty
Candlewick

Hubble's Universe (2014)
Terence Dickinson
Firefly Books

Space Encyclopedia: A Tour of Our Solar System and Beyond (2013)
David A. Aguilar
National Geographic Kids

The Planets (2014)
DK

50 Things You Should Know About Space (2016)
Raman Prinja
QEB Publishing

Websites

PowerKids Press has developed an online list of websites related to the subject of this book. This site is updated regularly. Please use this link to access the list:
www.powerkidslinks.com/pe/space

index